South Carolina, Mayfield W.D.

The School Law of South Carolina

Edition of 1896

South Carolina, Mayfield W.D.

The School Law of South Carolina
Edition of 1896

ISBN/EAN: 9783744666893

Printed in Europe, USA, Canada, Australia, Japan

Cover: Foto ©Suzi / pixelio.de

More available books at **www.hansebooks.com**

THE SCHOOL LAW

OF

SOUTH CAROLINA.

EDITION OF 1896.

Prepared and Published in Pursuance of Law, under the Direction of

W. D. MAYFIELD,

STATE SUPERINTENDENT OF EDUCATION.

COLUMBIA, S. C.
THE BRYAN PRINTING COMPANY.
1896.

The Provision of the State Constitution Relating to Education.

ARTICLE XI.

EDUCATION.

SECTION 1. The supervision of public instruction shall be vested in a State Superintendent of Education, who shall be elected for the term of two years by the qualified electors of the State, in such manner and at such time as the other State officers are elected; his powers, duties and compensation shall be defined by the General Assembly.

SEC. 2. There shall be a State Board of Education, composed of the Governor, the State Superintendent of Education, and not exceeding seven persons to be appointed by the Governor every four years, of which Board the Governor shall be Chairman, and the State Superintendent of Education, Secretary. This Board shall have the regulation of examination of teachers applying for certificates of qualification, and shall award all scholarships, and have such other powers and duties as may be determined by law. The traveling expenses of the persons to be appointed shall be provided for by the General Assembly.

SEC. 3. The General Assembly shall make provision for the election or appointment of all other necessary school officers, and shall define their qualifications, powers, duties, compensation and terms of office.

SEC. 4. The salaries of the State and County school officers and compensation of County Treasurers for collecting and disbursing school moneys shall not be paid out of the school funds, but shall be otherwise provided for by the General Assembly.

SEC. 5. The General Assembly shall provide for a liberal system of free public schools for all children between the ages of six and twenty-one years, and for the division of the Counties into suitable school districts, as compact in form as practicable, having regard to natural boundaries, and not to exceed forty-nine nor be less than nine square miles in area: *Provided,* That in cities of ten thousand inhabitants and over, this limitation of area shall not apply: *Provided, further,* That when any school district laid out under this Section shall embrace cities or towns already organized into special school districts in which graded school buildings have been erected by the issue of bonds, or by special taxation, or by donation, all the territory included in said school district shall bear its just proportion of any tax that may be levied to liquidate such bonds or support the public schools therein: *Provided, further*, That nothing in this Article contained shall be construed as a repeal of the laws under which the several graded school districts of this State are organized. The present division of the Counties into school districts and the provisions of law now governing the same, shall remain until changed by the General Assembly.

SEC. 6. The existing County Boards of Commissioners of the several Counties, or such officer or officers as may hereafter be vested with the same or similar powers and duties, shall levy an annual tax of three mills on the dollar upon all the taxable property in their respective Counties, which tax shall be collected at the same time and by the same officers as the other taxes for the same year, and shall be held in the County treasury of the respective Counties; and the said fund shall be apportioned among the school districts of the County in proportion to the number of pupils enrolled in the public schools of the respective districts, and the officer or officers charged by law with making said apportionment shall notify the Trustees of the respective school districts thereof, who shall expend and disburse the same as the General Assembly may prescribe. The General Assembly shall define "enrollment." Not less than three Trustees for each school district shall be selected from the qualified voters and taxpayers therein, in such manner and for such terms as the General Assembly may determine, except in cases of special school districts now existing, where the provisions of law now governing the same shall remain until changed by the General Assembly: *Provided*, The manner of the selection of said Trustees need not be uniform throughout the State. There shall be assessed on all taxable polls in the State, between the ages of twenty-one and sixty years (excepting Confederate soldiers above the age of fifty years), an annual tax of one dollar on each poll, the proceeds of which tax shall be expended for school purposes in the several school districts in which it is collected. Whenever during the three next ensuing fiscal years the tax levied by the said County Boards of Commissioners or similar officers and the poll tax shall not yield an amount equal to three dollars per capita of the number of children enrolled in the public schools of each County for the scholastic year ending the thirty-first day of October, in the year eighteen hundred and ninety-five, as it appears in the report of the State Superintendent of Education for said scholastic year, the Comptroller General shall, for the aforesaid three next ensuing fiscal years, on the first day of each of said years, levy such an annual tax on the taxable property of the State as he may determine to be necessary to make up such deficiency, to be collected as other State taxes, and apportion the same among the Counties of the State in proportion to the respective deficiencies therein. The sum so apportioned shall be paid by the State Treasurer to the County Treasurers of the respective Counties, in proportion to the respective deficiencies therein, on the warrant of the Comptroller General, and shall be apportioned among the school districts of the Counties, and disbursed as other school funds; and from and after the thirty-first day of December, in the year eighteen hundred and ninety-eight, the General Assembly shall cause to be levied annually on all the taxable property of the State such a tax, in addition to the said tax levied by the said County Boards of Commissioners or similar officers, and poll tax above provided, as may be necessary to keep the schools open throughout the State for such length of time in each scholastic year as the General Assembly may prescribe; and said tax shall be apportioned among the Counties in proportion to the deficiencies therein, and disbursed as other school funds. Any school district may, by the authority of the General Assembly, levy an additional tax for the support of its schools.

SEC. 7. Separate schools shall be provided for children of the white and colored races, and no child of either race shall ever be permitted to attend a school provided for children of the other race.

SEC. 8. The General Assembly may provide for the maintenance of Clemson Agricultural College, the University of South Carolina, and the Winthrop Normal and Industrial College, a branch thereof, as now established by law, and may create scholarships therein; the proceeds realized from the land scrip given by the act of Congress passed the second day of July, in the year eighteen hundred and sixty-two, for the support of an agricultural college, and any lands or funds which have heretofore been or may hereafter be given or appropriated for educational purposes by the Congress of the United States, shall be applied as directed in the Acts appropriating the same: *Provided*, That the General Assembly shall, as soon as practicable, wholly separate Claflin College from Claflin University, and provide for a separate corps of professors and instructors therein, representation to be given to men and women of the negro race; and it shall be the Colored Normal, Industrial, Agricultural and Mechanical College of this State.

SEC. 9. The property or credit of the State of South Carolina, or of any county, city, town, township, school district or other subdivision of the said State, or any public money, from whatever source derived, shall not, by gift, donation, loan, contract, appropriation, or otherwise, be used, directly or indirectly, in aid or maintenance of any college, school, hospital, orphan house, or other institution, society or organization, of whatever kind, which is wholly or in part under the direction or control of any church or of any religious or sectarian denomination, society or organization.

SEC. 10. All gifts of every kind for educational purposes, if accepted by the General Assembly, shall be applied and used for the purposes designated by the giver, unless the same be in conflict with the provisions of this Constitution.

SEC. 11. All gifts to the State where the purpose is not designated, all escheated property, the net assets or funds of all estates or copartnerships in the hands of the Courts of the State where there have been no claimants for the same within the last seventy years, and other money coming into the Treasury of the State by reason of the twelfth Section of an Act entitled "An Act to provide a mode of distribution of the moneys as direct tax from the citizens of this State by the United States in trust to the State of South Carolina," approved the twenty-fourth day of December, in the year eighteen hundred and ninety-one, together with such other means as the General Assembly may provide, shall be securely invested as the State School Fund, and the annual income thereof shall be apportioned by the General Assembly for the purpose of maintaining the public schools.

SEC. 12. All the net income to be derived by the State from the sale or license for the sale of spirituous, malt, vinous and intoxicating liquors and beverages, not including so much thereof as is now or may hereafter be allowed by law to go to the Counties and municipal corporations of the State, shall be applied annually in aid of the supplementary taxes provided for in the sixth Section of this Article; and if after said application there should be a surplus, it shall be devoted to public school purposes, and apportioned as the General Assembly may determine: *Provided, however,* That the said supplementary taxes shall only be levied when the net income aforesaid from the sale or license from the sale of alcoholic liquors or beverages are not sufficient to meet and equalize the deficiencies for which the said supplementary taxes are provided.

ACT OF 1896.

The Free Public School Law.

Be it enacted by the General Assembly of the State of South Carolina:

STATE SUPERINTENDENT OF EDUCATION.

SECTION 1. The State Superintendent of Education shall be elected at each general election, in the same manner as other State officers, and shall enter upon the duties of his office at the time prescribed by law. Before entering upon the duties of his office he shall give bond, for the use of the State of South Carolina in the penal sum of five thousand ($5,000) dollars, with good and sufficient sureties, to be approved by the Governor, conditioned for the faithful and impartial performance of the duties of his office; and he shall also, at the time of giving bond, take and subscribe the oath prescribed in Section 26 of Article III. of the Constitution of the State, which shall be endorsed upon the back of said bond, and the bond shall be filed with and preserved by the Secretary of State. The Superintendent of Education shall receive as compensation for his services the sum of nineteen hundred dollars per annum, payable monthly out of the State Treasury, and his traveling expenses, not exceeding three hundred dollars, shall be paid out of the State Treasury upon duly itemized accounts rendered by him.

SEC. 2. He shall have general supervision over all the schools of the State supported in whole or in part from the public school funds, and it shall be his duty to visit every County in the State as often as practicable for the purpose of inspecting the schools, awakening an interest favorable to the cause of education, and diffusing as widely as possible, by public addresses and personal communication with school officers, teachers, and parents, a knowledge of existing defects and of desirable improvements in the government and instruction of said schools. He shall secure, by and with the advice of the State Board of Education, uniformity in the use of text books throughout the free public schools of the State, and shall forbid the use of sectarian or partisan books and instruction in said schools. He shall prepare and transmit to the several County Superintendents of Education school registers, blank certificates, reports and such other suitable blanks, forms and printed instructions as may be necessary to aid school officers and teachers in making their reports and carrying into full effect the various provisions of the school laws of this

State, and shall cause the law relating to the free public schools, with such rules, regulations, forms, and instructions as shall be legally prescribed, to be printed, together with a suitable index, in pamphlet form, at the expense of the State, and he shall cause copies of the same to be transmitted to the several County Superintendents of Education for distribution. He shall collect in his office such school books, apparatuses, maps, and charts as can be obtained. He may certify copies of all papers filed in his office, and such certified copies shall be competent evidence thereof.

SEC. 3. He shall make a report, through the Governor, to the General Assembly at each regular session thereof, showing: 1st. The whole number of pupils registered in, and the number enrolled as hereinafter defined in, the free common schools of this State during the year ending the thirtieth day of the last preceding June, and the number in each County registered in, and the number enrolled as hereinafter defined in, during the same period. 2d. The number of whites and the number of colored of each sex attending the said schools. 3d. The number of free schools in the State. 4th. The number of pupils studying each of the branches taught. 5th. The average wages paid to teachers of each sex and to the principals of schools and departments in said schools. 6th. The number of school houses erected during the year, and the location, material and cost thereof. 7th. The number previously erected, and the material of their construction, and their condition and value, and the number with the grounds enclosed. 8th. The Counties in which Teachers' Institutes were held, and the number attending the institutes in each County. 9th. Such other statistical information as he may deem important, together with such plans as he may have matured and the State Board of Education may have recommended for the management and improvement of the school fund, and for the more perfect organization and efficiency of the free public schools. All State institutions of higher learning shall make an annual report, on or before the first day of September of each year, to the State Superintendent of Education, embracing a detailed account of the operations of such institutions, including the expenditure of the public moneys for the current scholastic year, which reports the State Superintendent of Education shall include in his annual report to the Legislature. All Acts or parts of Acts requiring annual reports to be made to other authorities are hereby repealed.

SEC. 4. The sum of nine hundred dollars shall be allowed to the State Superintendent of Education for the purpose of defraying the expenses of clerk hire in his office.

SEC. 5. The State Treasurer shall take and hold in trust for the

State any grant or devise of lands and any gift or bequest of money or other personal property made to him for educational purposes; all gifts to the State where the purpose is not designated; all escheated property; the net assets or funds of all estates or copartnerships in the hands of the Courts of the State where there have been no claimants for the same within the last seventy years, and other money coming into the Treasury of the State by reason of the twelfth Section of an Act entitled "An Act to provide a mode of distribution of the moneys as direct tax from the citizens of this State by the United States in trust to the State of South Carolina," approved the twenty-fourth day of December, in the year eighteen hundred and ninety-one, together with such other means as the General Assembly may provide. The State Treasurer shall, from time to time, invest in bonds of this State or of the United States all such money in the name of the State, as a permanent State school fund, and shall pay out the income derived therefrom to the County or Counties of the State as the same may be apportioned among said Counties by the State Board of Education: *Provided,* That no disposition shall be made of any property, grant, devise, gift or bequest inconsistent with the purposes, conditions or terms thereof. For the faithful management of all property so received by the State Treasurer, he shall be responsible, upon his bond, to the State as for other funds received by him in his official capacity: *Provided, however,* That the Trustees of any school district of this State may take and hold in trust for their particular school district any property granted, devised, given or bequeathed to such school district, and apply the same in the interest of the schools of their district in such manner as in their judgment seems most conducive to the welfare of the schools, when not otherwise directed by the terms of the grant, devise, gift or bequest: *And provided, further,* That before said Trustees shall assume control of any such grant, devise, gift or bequest, they shall give a bond, to be approved by the County Board of Education of the County in which such grant, devise, gift or bequest is made, conditioned for the faithful discharge of the trust reposed in them in respect to said property, which bond shall be deposited with the Clerk of the Court of said County. The said Trustees are hereby invested with the care and custody of all school houses or other school property belonging to their school districts, with full power to control the same in such manner as they may think will best subserve the interest of the free public schools and the cause of education.

SEC. 6. The State Superintendent of Education shall discharge such other duties as may be provided by law; and he shall deliver to his successor, within ten days after the expiration of his term of office, all books, papers, documents, and other property belonging to his office.

SEC. 7. In case a vacancy occurs in the office of State Superintendent of Education from any cause, such vacancy shall be filled by the Governor, by and with the advice and consent of the Senate, and the person so appointed shall qualify within fifteen days from the date of such appointment or else the office will be deemed vacant. If the vacancy occur during the recess of the Senate the Governor shall fill the same by appointment until the Senate can act thereon.

STATE BOARD OF EDUCATION.

SEC. 8. The Governor, the State Superintendent of Education, and seven persons, one from each Congressional District, to be appointed by the Governor, who shall hold office for four years and until their successors may be appointed, unless sooner removed by the Governor, shall constitute the State Board of Education. Of this Board the Governor shall be *ex officio* Chairman, and the State Superintendent of Education shall be Secretary of the Board. The Secretary shall be custodian of its records, papers, and effects, and shall keep minutes of its proceedings; and said records, papers, and minutes shall be kept in the office of the State Superintendent of Education, and shall be open to inspection by the public.

SEC. 9. The said Board shall meet on the call of its Chairman, or upon the request of a majority of its members, at the office of the State Superintendent of Education, or at such other place as may be designated in the call. A majority of the Board shall constitute a quorum for transacting business. The official seal of the State Superintendent of Education shall be used for the authentication of the acts of the State Board. The members of the State Board of Education appointed by the Governor shall receive as compensation the same mileage and per diem as is provided for members of the General Assembly, not exceeding twenty days in any one year.

SEC. 10. The State Board of Education shall constitute an advisory body, with whom the State Superintendent of Education shall have the right to consult when he is in doubt as to his official duty; and shall have power to review on appeal all decisions of the County Boards of Education, as hereinafter provided for. Appeals to the State Board of Education must be made through the County Boards of Education in writing, and must distinctly set forth the question of law as well as the facts of the case upon which the appeal is taken, and the decision of the State Board shall be final upon the matter at issue.

SEC. 11. The State Board of Education shall have power: 1st.

To adopt rules and regulations not inconsistent with the laws of the State for its own government and for the government of the free public schools. 2d. To prescribe and enforce rules for the examination of teachers. 3d. To prescribe a standard of proficiency before County Boards of Education which will entitle persons examined by such Boards to certificates as teachers. 4th. To prescribe and enforce the course of study in the free public schools. 5th. To prescribe and to enforce, as far as practicable, the use of a uniform series of text books in the free public schools of the State; to enter into an agreement with the publishers of the books prescribed, fixing the time of prescription and the price above which the books shall not be retailed during the period of prescription, and a rate of discount at not less than which the books shall be furnished to the retail dealers in this State; to require the publishers, in the discretion of the Board, to establish in each County one or more depositories of their books within the State at such place or places as the Board may designate and where such books may be obtained without delay; and to exact of the publishers a bond in the sum of not more than five thousand dollars conditioned for the faithful performance of the agreement, and with a penalty of twenty-five dollars for each violation of the agreement, the form and execution of the bond to be approved by the Attorney General of the State, which agreement and bond shall be deposited with the State Treasurer, all recoveries thereon to go into the State Treasury for school purposes: *Provided*, That the State Board of Education shall not have power, without permission of the General Assembly of the State, to change a text book within five (5) years from the date of its adoption, except for violation of the agreement entered into by its publisher with the State Board of Education, for which cause it may be changed by the said Board, and it shall be unlawful for any teacher drawing public school money to use any book not prescribed by the State Board of Education, without the consent, in writing, of said Board. 6th. To grant State teachers' certificates, and to revoke them for immoral or unprofessional conduct, profanity or evident unfitness for teaching. 7th. To review on appeal an order revoking a County certificate: *Provided*, That no certificate be required of examination or proficiency from any applicant for teachers in city schools of Charleston having diplomas from the Memminger Normal School in the city of Charleston, whether regular or extra teachers, but they shall be alone subjected to such examinations and conditions as may be required by the Board of Commissioners of the city public schools of Charleston. 8th. To award scholarships created by the General Assembly in the institutions of learning supported in whole or in part by the State.

SEC. 12. No child shall be counted in the enrollment more than once, nor in more than one school district in any one school year, and the school officer charged with the duty of enrollment willfully violating this provision shall be guilty of a misdemeanor. The teacher or principal of every school shall keep and furnish annually to the Trustees of the School District a list of all pupils that have attended the school during the preceding scholastic year, showing the names of the pupils, their respective places of residence, and the number of days each pupil has attended, which list shall be certified to the County Board of Education by said Trustees on or before the 1st day of August in every year.

COUNTY SUPERINTENDENT OF EDUCATION.

SEC. 13. At the expiration of the terms of office of the School Commissioners of the several Counties of the State there shall be elected by the qualified electors of the County a County Superintendent of Education for each County, who shall hold his office for the term of two years and until his successor is elected and qualified. He shall, before being commissioned and entering upon the duties of his office, give bond to the State, for the use of the County in which he is elected for educational purposes, in the penal sum of one thousand dollars, with good and sufficient sureties, to be approved by the County Board of Commissioners, conditioned for the faithful and impartial discharge of the duties of his office, and shall take and subscribe the oath of office prescribed in Section 26, Article III., of the Constitution of this State, which he shall file in the office of the Secretary of State. When commissioned he shall immediately enter upon the discharge of his duties. His failure to qualify within thirty days after notice of his election shall create a vacancy.

SEC. 14. The State Board of Education shall fill all vacancies in the office of County Superintendent of Education for the unexpired term.

SEC. 15. The salary of the County Superintendent of Education of each County shall be the same as that now fixed or hereafter to be fixed by law for the School Commissioner thereof, except in Chester County, in which the salary shall be five hundred dollars, payable monthly, by the County Board of Commissioners, out of the ordinary County funds; and he shall be allowed one hundred dollars per annum for traveling expenses, if so much be necessary, payable in the same manner, upon an itemized statement of such expenses being filed with said Board: *Provided,* Nothing shall be allowed for traveling expenses in the Counties of Saluda, Edgefield, Darlington, and Berkeley.

SEC. 16. It shall be the duty of each County Superintendent of Education to visit the schools in his County at least once in each year, and oftener if practicable, and to note the course and method of instruction and the branches taught, and to give such recommendation, in the art of teaching and the method thereof, in each school as shall be necessary, so that uniformity in the course of studies and method of instruction employed shall be secured, as far as practicable, in the schools of the several grades respectively. He shall acquaint himself, as far as practicable, with the character and condition of each school, noting any deficiencies that may exist, either in the government of the school or the classification of its pupils or the method of instruction employed in the several branches, and shall make such suggestions in private to the teachers as to him shall appear necessary to the good order of the school and the progress of the pupils. He shall note the character and condition of the school houses, the sufficiency or insufficiency of the furniture, and shall make such suggestions to the several Boards of Trustees as in his opinion shall seem conducive to the comfort and progress of the several schools. It shall be the duty of each County Superintendent of Education to aid the teachers in all proper efforts to improve themselves in their profession. For this purpose he shall encourage the formation of associations of teachers for common improvement and conduct teachers' institutes. He shall attend the meetings of such associations and give such advice and instruction in regard to their conduct and management as in his judgment will contribute to their greater efficiency.

SEC. 17. The County Superintendent of Education shall attend the annual settlements of the County Treasurer with the Comptroller General.

SEC. 18. The annual report of the County Superintendent of Education shall contain the complete statistics of all schools within his County supported in whole or in part from the public funds, as may be required of him by the State Superintendent of Education.

SEC. 19. The County Superintendent of Education shall make an annual report of all claims filed, audited, allowed and ordered paid by him during each school year to the presiding Judge at the second term of the Court of General Sessions for each County which shall be held after the first day of January in each year, which report shall be submitted by said Judge to the Grand Jury for their examination: *Provided,* That after examination the Grand Jury shall report thereon to the presiding Judge any matter growing out of or pertaining to said annual report, which to them may seem worthy of the attention of the Court. The said report shall thereupon be filed by the Clerk of said Court and kept as papers of said Court for inspection by any citizen desirous of examining the same.

SEC. 20. The County Board of Commissioners of each County are authorized and required to furnish the County Superintendent of Education of their County with a comfortable and convenient office and suitable office furniture, and to supply said office with fuel, lights, stationery, postage, and such other incidentals as are necessary to the proper transaction of the legitimate business of his office.

SEC. 21. It shall be the duty of the County Superintendent of Education, on or before the fifteenth day of July in each year, to report to the County Treasurer by school districts all school claims approved by him for the school year last preceding, and the County Treasurer shall thereupon close the school accounts for that year, carrying over any balance to the credit of each school district of the then current fiscal year.

SEC. 22. The County Superintendent of Education shall keep a register of all claims approved by him and of such other matters as the State Superintendent of Education shall require of him and in the form prescribed by the State Superintendent.

SEC. 23. The County Superintendent of Education shall furnish the School Trustees of his County with copies of the reports made to him by the County Auditor and County Treasurer as to the persons listed and paying poll tax, and shall aid the Trustees in making all proper corrections.

SEC. 24. The County Superintendent of Education shall keep in his office a die, in a circular form, upon the centre of which shall be engraved in capital letters the word "seal," and on the circumference the proper words indicating the office, which shall be regarded as the seal of the office, and which the County Superintendent of Education shall be required to impress upon all papers issued from his office, and affix his name to such paper. And it shall be the duty of the County Board of Commissioners in each County to furnish the County Superintendent of Education of their respective Counties with such seal.

COUNTY BOARD OF EDUCATION.

SEC. 25. There shall be a County Board of Education in each County, composed of the County Superintendent of Education and two other persons of such County, to be appointed by the State Board of Education, who shall hold their office for the term of two years from the time of their appointment, and until their successors shall be qualified, unless sooner removed by the State Board of Education. No person shall be appointed a member of the "County Board of Education" unless he is qualified to hold a first grade certificate.

SEC. 26. The County Board of Education shall examine all candidates for the position of teacher, and give to each person found qualified a certificate setting forth the branches of learning he or she may be capable of teaching, and the percentage attained in each branch; said certificate to be valid for a term of two years, unless sooner revoked, and it may be renewed with or without examination, at the discretion of the Board, all of which shall be done under such regulations as the State Board of Education may prescribe. No teacher shall be employed in any of the free public schools without a certificate from the County Board of Education or the State Board of Education: *Provided*, That no examination as to qualification shall be made in the case of any applicant who produces a full diploma from any chartered college or university of this State or Memminger Normal School of Charleston, and furnishes satisfactory evidence of good moral character. The two members of the Board appointed by the State Board of Education shall receive for the services rendered by them compensation at the rate of three dollars per diem for not exceeding seven days in each year, and mileage of five cents for each mile of necessary travel, the same to be paid by the County Board of Commissioners out of the ordinary County funds.

SEC. 27. It shall be the duty of the County Board of Education and of the Boards of Trustees hereinafter provided for to see that in every school under their care there shall be taught, as far as practicable, orthography, reading, writing, arithmetic, geography, English grammar, the elements of agriculture, history of the United States and of this State, the principles of the Constitution, and laws of the United States and of this State, morals and good behavior, algebra, physiology, and hygiene, and especially as to the effects of alcoholic liquors and narcotics upon the human system, English literature, and such other branches as the State Board may from time to time direct.

SEC. 28. The County Boards of Education of the several Counties of this State shall levy an annual tax of three mills on the dollar upon all the taxable property in their respective Counties, which tax shall be collected at the same time and by the same officers as the other taxes for the same year, and shall be held in the County treasury of the respective Counties; and on the first day of July of each year, or as soon as practicable thereafter, the said fund shall be apportioned by the said County Boards respectively among the school districts of their respective Counties in proportion to the number of pupils enrolled in the public schools of such school districts; and the said County Boards shall ascertain the amount of poll taxes collected in and for each school district of their respective Counties, and shall notify the County Treasurer and the Trustees of each school district of the amount of such poll taxes, as well as of the amount of the aforesaid fund apportioned by them to each school district. The school funds of each school district shall be distributed and expended by the Board of Trustees for the best interest of the school district, according to the judgment of the Board of Trustees, on their warrant approved by the County Superintendent of Education. For the purpose of said apportionment, pupils shall not be deemed enrolled until after an attendance of at least ten school days during the preceding scholastic year: *Provided*, That the apportionment of funds until the expiration of the fiscal year 1896 shall be as now provided by law.

SEC. 29. The County Board of Education shall constitute an advisory body, with whom the County Superintendent of Education shall have the right to consult when he is in doubt as to his official duty, and also a tribunal for determining any matter of local controversy in reference to the construction or administration of the school laws, with the power to summon witnesses and take testimony if necessary; and when they have made a decision said decision shall be binding upon the parties to the controversy: *Provided*, That either of the parties shall have the right to appeal to the State Board of Education, and said appeal shall be made through the County Board of Education in writing, and shall distinctly set forth the question in dispute, the decision of the County Board, and the testimony as agreed upon by the parties to the controversy, or, if they fail to agree, upon the testimony as reported by the County Board.

SEC. 30. The County Board of Education shall meet for the purpose of examining applicants for teacher's certificates and the transaction of other business, at least twice a year, at such places and at such times as the State Board of Education shall appoint. The County Superintendent shall be Chairman and Clerk of the Board, and shall keep a fair record of their proceedings, and register of the name, age, sex, color, residence and date of certificate of each person to whom a certificate is issued, and in case the certificate be cancelled, shall make a proper entry of the same. The Board shall have power to revoke any certificate granted by them, for immoral or improper conduct or evident unfitness for teaching. The Board shall hold as many additional meetings during the year as the interest of the free public schools of the County may require, subject to regulations, prescribed by the State Board of Education.

SEC. 31. The County Boards of Education shall divide their Counties into convenient school districts, as compact in form as practicable, having regard to natural boundaries, and not to exceed forty-nine nor be less than nine square miles in area: *Provided,* That in cities of ten thousand inhabitants and over, this limitation of area shall not apply: *Provided, further,* That when any school district laid out under this Section shall embrace cities or towns already organized into special school districts in which graded school buildings have been erected by the issue of bonds, or by special taxation, or by donation, all the territory included in said school district shall bear its just proportion of any tax that may be levied to liquidate such bonds or support the public schools therein. The present division of the Counties into school districts shall remain until changed by the County Boards of Education. The County Boards of Education are authorized and empowered to make contracts for the purpose of dividing their Counties into proper school districts, and to provide for the payment of the expenses thereof out of the school funds of the County. Every school district now organized or to be hereafter organized in pursuance of this Section is, and shall be, a body politic and corporate, by the name and style of School District No. ——— (such number as may be designated by the County Board of Education), of ————— County (the name of the County in which the district is situated), the State of South Carolina, and in that name may sue and be sued, and be capable of contracting and being contracted with to the extent of their school fund, and holding such real and personal estate as it may come into possession of by will or otherwise, or as is authorized by law to be purchased, all of which shall be used exclusively for school purposes.

SEC. 32. Each school district shall be under the management and control of the Board of Trustees hereinafter provided for, subject to the supervision of the County Board of Education.

SEC. 33. The school districts of the several Counties of the State are hereby made and declared to be the divisions of the Counties for taxation for all school purposes.

SEC. 34. That the voters of any school district who return real or personal property of the value of one hundred dollars for taxation are authorized to levy and collect an annual tax to supplement any Constitutional or other tax for like purposes, and all electors voting in such election imposing such extra levy of tax for school purposes shall exhibit their tax receipts and registration certificates as required in other general elections, and for said purposes the Trus-
2—SL

tees of said school districts, upon the written request of six resident freeholders of the age of twenty-one years, shall call a public meeting of said taxpayers at any time before the first day of June of any fiscal year, which meeting must be advertised in a newspaper published in such city, incorporated town or village once a week for two weeks, or posted in three conspicuous places in such school district for said length of time, and when assembled a ballot shall be had, and if a majority shall vote to levy such special tax, not exceeding four mills, the Trustees shall, after having notice of same posted in at least three public places within the district for not less than ten days, order an election, at which election only such taxpayers as above mentioned shall vote, that within ten days after such election, if a majority of those voting shall vote for such levy, the Board of Trustees shall furnish the County Auditor with a statement of the amount so levied and the Auditor shall enter the same in the tax duplicates, and he shall annually each year.thereafter enter said amount in the tax duplicate until the same is increased, decreased or repealed by said taxpayers, at a meeting called for that purpose, and he is notified that the same is increased, decreased or repealed, and, if increased or decreased, he shall annually enter it as before, which meeting shall be called and notice given in the same way and manner as is herein provided for the calling of meetings to make the levy, and the giving of the notice that it has been made, and the County Treasurer shall collect the same as other County and State taxes; such levy shall be a lien on the property in such school district which shall be subject thereto in case of default of payment. That said tax so collected shall be paid out by the County Treasurer upon warrants drawn by the Board of Trustees, countersigned by the County Superintendent of Education: *Provided*, That any surplus of such levy remaining in the hands of the County Treasurer at the expiration of any fiscal year shall be paid out as other school funds of the district. Each taxpayer, when he pays any taxes for school purposes voted under the provisions of this Section, shall have the right to designate to which school in said school district he wishes the money paid by him to go, and the Treasurer shall keep a note of such designation, and the money be applied as thus designated. When no designation is made by the taxpayer at the time of such payment, the money shall be expended as other school funds in such district: *Provided*, That nothing herein contained shall be construed to change the manner now provided by law for the collection and paying out of special taxes in any school district now established by any special Act of the General Assembly and organized thereunder.

SEC. 35. That whenever it shall happen that, by reason of the location of special school districts, portions of two adjacent Counties should, for convenience be included in one school district, the County Boards of Education of such Counties are hereby authorized and directed in joint conference to make such regulations as will enable such sections to be established into a separate school district.

TRUSTEES.

SEC. 36. Each County Board of Education, on the first Tuesday of July, 1896, and on the first Tuesday of July every two years thereafter, shall appoint for each school district in their County three School Trustees from the qualified electors and taxpayers residing within the district, who shall hold their office for two years and until their successors are appointed and qualified, unless sooner removed by the County Board of Education. The County Board of Education shall have power to fill, from time to time, all vacancies in Boards of Trustees. The School Trustees shall meet as a Board as soon and as often as practicable after having been appointed and qualified, at such place as may be most convenient in the district, and at their first meeting they shall organize by electing one of their number Chairman of the Board, who shall preside at the official meeting of the Board, and another Clerk of the Board, who shall record their proceedings in a book provided for that purpose. Each member of the Board of Trustees shall be duly notified of all meetings of the Board by the Clerk of the Board. The terms of office of all Trustees now in office shall expire on the 30th day of June, 1896: *Provided*, That the foregoing provisions of this Section shall not apply to special and graded school districts created by special Acts, but that the Trustees and School Commissioners of all special and graded school districts shall remain the same in number, and shall be elected or appointed in the same manner, and shall hold office for the same time as is provided for in the respective special Acts, except that in the special school districts where the Trustees or their successors are appointed by the State Superintendent of Education under the provisions of the special Acts the Trustees shall hold office until the first Tuesday in July, 1896, on which day, and on the same day every two years thereafter, the Trustees shall be elected by the qualified electors of such school district. The election for all Trustees for all such school districts shall be by ballot, and shall be conducted under the supervision of three qualified electors residing within the district, who shall be appointed by the County Board of Education at least ten days prior to the holding of the election. The manager shall report the result of the election to the County Board of Education within ten days thereafter, which Board shall commission the Trustees so elected. The Board of Trustees of each special or graded school district shall elect from their number a Chairman, who shall preside at their meetings, and a Secretary, or a Secretary and Treasurer, who shall record the proceedings of the Board, and who shall keep a full and accurate account of all moneys received and expended, showing the source and disposition of each item, and who shall make a complete itemized report of the receipts and disbursements for each scholastic year to the County Superintendent of Education on or before the 15th day of July of each year. The books and vouchers of the Secretary and Treasurer shall be open at all times to inspection by the public.

No Trustees of any public school district or any special or graded school district shall be a Trustee of or stockholder in any private or other school or institution for higher education in this State.

SEC. 37. The Board of Trustees in each school district shall take the management and control of the local educational interests of the same, and shall visit each school in their district at least once in every school term, and shall be subject to the supervision and orders of the County Board of Education.

SEC. 38. The Board of Trustees shall hold a regular session in their school district at least two weeks before the commencement of any or every school term, for the transaction of any and all business necessary to the prosperity of the schools, with power to adjourn from time to time, and to hold special meetings at any time or place when called upon by the Chairman or any two members of the Board.

SEC. 39. The School Trustees of the several school districts are authorized and empowered to sell any school property, real or personal, in their school districts whenever they deem it expedient to do so, and to apply the proceeds of sale or sales to the school fund of the district wherein such sale is made: *Provided*, That the consent of the County Board of Education be first obtained by the Trustees desiring to make such sale.

That it shall be the duty of the said Board of Trustees within thirty days after said sale to enclose a report of the same to the County Board of Education, setting forth the terms and amount of said sale.

SEC. 40. When it shall so happen that persons are so situated as to be better accommodated at the school of an adjoining school district, whether special or otherwise, the Board of Trustees of the school district in which such persons reside may transfer such persons for education to the school district in which such school is located; and the Trustees of the school district where the school is located may receive such persons into the school as though they resided within the district upon such terms as may be agreed: *Provided*, That children shall not be transferred from a school district in one County to a school district in an adjoining County without the consent of the Board of Education of the respective Counties in which the transfer is made: *Provided, further*, That if any taxpayer pays taxes in two or more Counties, he shall have the right to send his children to the schools of any one of such Counties.

SEC. 41. Each school teacher shall make out and file with the Clerk of the Board of Trustees, at the expiration of each school month, a full and complete report of the whole number of pupils admitted to the school during each month, distinguishing between male and female, the average attendance, the branches taught, the number of pupils engaged in studying each of said branches, and such statistics as he or she may be required to make by the County Board of Education: *Provided*, That whenever a teacher is unavoidably prevented from filing said report at the expiration of any school month, the Board of School Trustees may have authority to receive the report within a reasonable time thereafter, if in their opinion the reasons for the delay are good and sufficient. On the filing of the teacher's report, and its approval by the Board of Trustees, their clerk shall draw an order in duplicate on the County Treasurer for the amount due such teacher, which shall be signed by the Board, which order, if accompanied by a copy of said monthly report, and approved by the County Superintendent of Education, shall be countersigned by him and the duplicate filed in his office.

SEC. 42. All claims, of every description whatever, which are chargeable against the fund raised for the support of the free public schools of the State, except such as are otherwise provided for by law, must be signed by at least a majority of the Board of Trustees of the school district against which the claims are chargeable; and the correctness and legality of the same shall be sworn to and sub-scribed by the person presenting such claim, before it shall be approved by the person or persons authorized by law to give such approval. School Trustees and County Superintendents of Education shall, free of charge, administer oaths to persons presenting the claims contemplated by this Section.

SEC. 43. It shall be unlawful for a School Trustee to receive pay as a teacher of a free public school.

SEC. 44. The Board of Trustees shall also have authority, and it shall be their duty: 1st. To provide suitable school houses in their districts, and to make the same comfortable, paying due regard to any school house already built or site procured, as well as to all

other circumstances [proper to be considered, so as best to promote
the educational interests of their district. 2d. To employ teachers
from those having certificates from their County Board of Examiners, or from the State Board of Education, and fix their salaries,
and to discharge the same when good and sufficient reasons for so
doing present themselves, subject to the supervision of the County
Board of Education. 3d. To suspend or dismiss pupils when the
best interests of the schools make it necessary. 4th. To call meetings of the qualified electors of the district for consultation in regard
to the school interests thereof, at which meetings the Chairman or
other member of the Board shall preside if present. 5th. To take
care of, manage, and control the school property of the district.
6th. To·visit the free public schools within their district from time
to time, and to take care that they are conducted according to law
and with the utmost efficiency. 7th. They shall be allowed to cross
all bridges or ferries free of charge when they are traveling on
official business.

MISCELLANEOUS.

SEC. 45. The County Auditor shall require each taxpayer to return
the number and name of the school district in which he resides
when he makes his tax return, and the Auditor shall state the same
in a separate column in the tax duplicates.

SEC. 46. The County Auditor, when he has completed the tax
duplicates, shall report to the County Superintendent of Education
by school districts the names listed for poll tax and the amount of
taxable property where there is a special levy.

SEC. 47. The several County Treasurers shall retain all the poll
tax collected in their respective Counties, and it is hereby made the
duty of the said County Treasurer in collecting the poll tax to keep
an account of the exact amount of said tax collected in each school
district in his County, and the poll tax collected therein shall be
expended for school purposes in the school district from which it
was collected; and any violation of this Section by the County
Treasurer shall constitute, and is hereby declared, a misdemeanor,
and on conviction thereof the said County Treasurer shall pay a fine
of not more than five hundred dollars, to be used for school purposes in the County suffering from such violation, or imprisonment,
in the discretion of the court.

SEC. 48. That each County Treasurer, when he has finished the
collection of taxes for his County, shall report to the County Superintendent of Education the names of the persons in the respective
school districts who have paid their poll tax.

SEC. 49. It shall be the duty of each County Treasurer to report monthly, on the fifteenth day of each month, to the County Superintendent of Education of his County, the amount of collections and disbursements made by him for the month on account of school tax and all other school funds; and it shall be a misdemeanor, on the part of any County Treasurer, to neglect, fail, or refuse to make such report, and on conviction thereof he shall pay a fine of not more than five hundred dollars, the same to be used for school purposes in his County.

SEC. 50. All moneys disbursed by any County Treasurer on account of school funds, taxes or other school funds, shall be paid on the orders of the Board of School Trustees, countersigned by the County Superintendent of Education, or as otherwise directed by law.

SEC. 51. Each County Treasurer shall make out and forward to the State Superintendent of Education annually, on the first day of November, a certified statement showing by school districts the amount of poll tax and the amount of all other school taxes collected by him for the fiscal year ending on the 31st day of December next preceding; and should any County Treasurer fail, or neglect, or refuse to make and forward the statement as herein required, the State Superintendent of Education shall make a written complaint to the Circuit Solicitor for the County in which the said Treasurer resides, who shall prosecute the said County Treasurer for the same; and, on conviction thereof, he shall be subject to a fine of not more than five hundred dollars, the same to be used for free public school purposes in his County.

SEC. 52. The County Treasurer shall carry forward all sums in his hands collected for any previous year or years for school purposes and unexpended to the next fiscal year, and credit the same to the school district respectively for which it was apportioned, and he shall report the same to the County Superintendent of Education.

SEC. 53. It shall be unlawful for any County Treasurer, County Auditor, member of County Board of Education, or School Trustee to buy, discount or shave, directly or indirectly, or be in any way interested in, any teacher's pay certificate or other order on the school fund, except such as are payable to him for his own services. If any of the officers above said shall violate the provisions of this Section, he shall be deemed guilty of a misdemeanor, and, on conviction thereof, shall pay a fine of not less than five hundred dollars nor more than two thousand dollars, to be used for school purposes in his County, and shall be imprisoned at the discretion of the Court, or either or both, and shall forfeit the amount of such claim or of his interest in such claim; and the County Board of Education shall regulate the opening and closing of the school terms so as best to promote and subserve the educational interest of the different sections of their Counties: *Provided*, That all contracts which Boards of Trustees may make in excess of the funds apportioned to their district shall be void.

SEC. 54. It shall not be lawful for any person who is less than six or more than twenty-one years of age to attend any of the free public schools of this State.

SEC. 55. The members of the State Board of Education appointed by the Governor, members of the County Boards of Education appointed by the State Board of Education, and members of the Board of Trustees, shall be exempt from militia duty, and members of the Boards of Trustees shall also be exempt from road duty.

SEC. 56. If a member of any County Board of Education in any County of the State, or a Trustee of any school district, shall attempt to act or discharge the duties of either of said offices after he shall have been removed, or after his successor shall have qualified, he shall be deemed guilty of a misdemeanor, and after conviction be punished by a fine of not less than one hundred and one dollars or imprisonment for not less than thirty-one days, or both, at the discretion of the Court.

SEC. 57. That it shall be unlawful for any teacher of a school supported in whole or in part from the public school funds of this State, or any Trustee of any such school, or any other school officer, to become an active or silent agent of any school-book publisher, or be in any wise pecuniarily interested in the introduction of any school book or books into any school in this State. Any person violating any of the provisions hereof shall upon conviction thereof be deemed guilty of a misdemeanor, and be subject to a fine of not less than one hundred dollars or imprisonment in the County jail for a period of not less than thirty days, or both, at the discretion of the Circuit Judge.

SEC. 58. It shall be unlawful for pupils of one race to attend the schools provided by Boards of Trustees for persons of another race.

SEC. 59. That should the amount raised by the three mill tax and the poll tax and the net income to the State from the sale or license for the sale of alcoholic liquors, for school purposes, not yield, at any time within the next three fiscal years, beginning with January 1st, 1896, an amount equal to three dollars per capita of the number of children enrolled in the public schools of each County for the scholastic year ending October 31, 1895, as it appears in the report of the State Superintendent of Education for such scholastic year, the Comptroller General shall, for the three next ensuing fiscal years, on the first day of each year, levy such an annual tax on the taxable property of the State as he may determine to be necessary to make up such deficiency, to be collected in the same manner as other State taxes, and apportion the same among the Counties of the State in proportion to the respective deficiencies therein. The sum so apportioned shall be paid by the State Treasurer to the County Treasurers of the respective Counties in proportion to their respective deficiencies therein, on the warrant of the Comptroller General, and it shall be apportioned among the school districts of the Counties, and be disbursed as other school funds. And from and after the 31st day of December, 1898, the General Assembly shall cause to be levied annually on all the taxable property of the State such a tax, in addition to the three mill tax and poll tax, together with the net income for school purposes from the sale or license for the sale of alcoholic liquors, as may be necessary to keep the schools open throughout the State for a period not less than five months in each scholastic year, such tax to be apportioned among the Counties in proportion to their deficiencies, and be disbursed as other school funds.

SEC. 60. The scholastic year shall begin on the first day of July of each year and end on the thirtieth day of June following.

SEC. 61. The State Superintendent of Education may advertise for bids for all printing required under this Act, and shall let the same to the lowest bidder therefor, who shall be required to file with his bid a bond in double the amount of his bid for the faithful performance of the contract.

SEC. 62. Nothing contained in this Act shall be construed to repeal the Acts of the General Assembly creating special and graded school districts. And the provisions of said Acts shall apply to said school districts, except the special graded school district in the town of Blacksburg, which shall come under the provisions of this Act: *Provided*, That the Trustees of said school districts and Commissioners of the city schools of Charleston shall make annual reports to the State Superintendent of Education, in such form and at such time as he shall prescribe: *Provided, further*, Whenever under the provisions of law any municipal corporation is authorized to levy a special tax for the support of public schools therein, any person not a resident of said municipal corporation shall be entitled to a credit upon fees for the tuition of his or her children to the amount of such special tax paid by such person.

SEC. 63. That the provisions of Article 7, Chapter XXV., Title IX. of Volume 1 of the Revised Statutes, relating to the city of Charleston and the schools therein, being 1091 and 1094, inclusive, are hereby re-enacted and confirmed: *Provided*, That no general or special school trustees shall hereafter employ any teacher who has not a certificate to teach in the free public schools of the State. This provision, however, not to affect the employment of any teacher now teaching in any of the schools of the special school districts: *Provided, further,* That the Trustees of any such school shall always have the right and power to impose any additional examinations and qualifications they may deem proper before or after employing any teachers: *Provided, also,* That all funds of the free public schools of this State, other than those arising from the special levy of special school districts, shall be paid out of the County Treasury upon warrants duly vouched by the School Trustees of the respective schools or school districts or otherwise as provided by the laws governing any special school district.

SEC. 64. The Trustees, officers or persons in charge of all literary, scientific or professional institutions of learning incorporated, supported or aided by the State, of all schools or private educational institutions shall, on or before the 15th day of July in each year, make a report in writing to the State Superintendent of Education of such statistics as the Superintendent shall prescribe, relating to the number of pupils and instructors, courses of study, cost of tuition, and the general condition of the institution or school under their charge.

SEC. 65. The Superintendent shall prepare blank forms of inquiry for such statistics, and shall send the same to every such institution or school on or before the 10th day of May in each year, and so much of said information as he may deem proper be incorporated in his annual report.

SCHOLARSHIPS IN WINTHROP NORMAL AND INDUSTRIAL COLLEGE.

SECTION 1. The Board of Trustees of the Winthrop Normal and Industrial College shall have the authority to assign the scholarships provided for that institution by the General Assembly so that there may be given to a County as many scholarships as such County is entitled to members in the House of Representatives, at forty-four dollars each instead of one scholarship at one hundred and fifty dollars as at present. These scholarships shall be awarded upon competative examination by the State Board of Education.

SEC. 2. That all Acts and parts of Acts contrary to this Act shall be, and the same are hereby, repealed.

RULES AND REGULATIONS CONCERNING PEABODY SCHOLARSHIPS IN THE PEABODY NORMAL COLLEGE, AT NASHVILLE, TENN.

I. The intent of the Peabody Board of Trust in establishing these scholarships in the Normal College is to affect public education in the South through a high grade of professionally educated teachers.

1. The realization of this intent implies, on the part of teachers: high moral aims; natural aptness to teach; an education of the liberal type; a knowledge of the history, theory and art of education; and the pursuit of teaching as a vocation.

II. A Peabody Scholarship is worth $100 a year, and railroad expenses to and from college one time, and is good for two years. The college year consists of eight months, beginning on the first Wednesday in October and closing on the last Wednesday in May, and scholarship students receive from the President of the College $12.50 at the end of each of these eight months.

1. No payment will be made except for time of actual attendance.

2. Scholarships will be withdrawn from students who allow bills for board to go unpaid.

III. These scholarships are distributed to the several States by the General Agent, and are awarded to students through the State Superintendents of their respective States. The whole number of scholarships is 114, and they are distributed at present as follows:

Alabama,·13; Arkansas, 10; Georgia, 14; Louisiana, 8; North Carolina, 14; South Carolina, 14; Tennessee, 14; Texas, 9; Virginia, 14; West Virginia, 8.

1. No State can claim scholarships as a right. They are gifts from the Peabody Board of Trust, and as such the ratio of their distribution, as well as their amount, may be changed, or they may be withheld altogether.

2. At the close of each college year the President will notify State Superintendents of the vacancies which are to be filled in their respective States for the ensuing college year.

IV. Scholarships are awarded on competitive examination, and persons who desire to compete for them should make application as early as June 1 to their State Superintendent, who will forward information as to the time and place of examination.

1. When State Superintendents cannot conduct these competitive examinations in person, they should be careful to delegate this duty to competent hands.

2. There would be a manifest advantage in selecting the same date for these examinations in the several States. The first week in August is suggested.

3. Only two years of scholarship aid will be given to the same student.

V. For the purpose of securing to all applicants a uniform basis of competition, the questions for examination will be prepared by the President of the College and sent to the State Superintendents for distribution to the examiners whom they may appoint.

1. These questions, with specific instructions for their use, should be sent to the examiners in sealed envelopes, which are not to be opened till the hour for examination has come.

2. Each competitor should be required to return the lists of printed questions to the examiners as soon as the answers have been written.

VI. The qualifications for becoming a competitor for a scholarship are as follows: The applicant must be not less than seventeen years of age, nor more than thirty; irreproachable moral character; good health; no physical defects, habits, or eccentricities, which would interfere with success in teaching; a purpose to follow teaching as a vocation.

1. The task of the examiners will be simplified by making a preliminary examination as suggested above.

2. Preference should be given to young men who do not use tobacco in any form.

3. If it should appear that a candidate intends to use his scholarship chiefly as a means of securing an education, or of ultimately preparing himself for some profession other than teaching, he should not be allowed to compete.

4. Persons of sluggish or indolent temperaments, of slovenly habits, or of vicious disposition, should be at once rejected.

5. When a choice must be made between a young man and a young woman whose examination papers are of equal merit, the young man should be preferred.

VII. The minimum literary qualifications for securing a scholarship are the following: The ability to read fluently, to write a fair hand, to spell correctly, and to express thoughts in grammatical English; to solve problems of moderate difficulty under all the ordinary rules of arithmetic, and to demonstrate any ordinary arithmetical principle; to locate the principal cities, rivers, and mountains of the world, and to give the boundaries of any specified State of the Union; to parse the words of any ordinary English sentence, and to correct ungrammatical English; to solve equations of two unknown quantities; to describe the leading events in the history of the United States. *The standard for entrance will be raised from year to year.*

1. In the main, the examinations should be written, but certain intellectual qualities can best be tested in the oral way.

2. The ability to think and to reason is of more importance than mere attainment of facts and rules. General intelligence and brightness may offset some deficiencies in mere book-learning.

3. Good breeding, politeness and a pleasant manner should be counted in a candidate's favor.

VIII. A scholarship is good for any two consecutive years above the Freshman Class; that is, for Sophomore and Junior, or for Junior and Senior, or for Senior and Post-Graduate.

1. When scholarship students reach the College, they will not be re-examined for admission.

2. As the number of scholarships is small compared with the number of competitors, it will often happen that some of those who miss the prize are competent to enter the Sophomore Class of the College. When persons of this class desire to enter the College, they will, on application, receive from their State Superintendent a SPECIAL CERTIFICATE, which will admit them to the College without further examination. *This Certificate has no money value.*

3. Students who have gained admittance to the Sophomore Class have the privilege of being examined for any of the higher classes. Candidates are recommended to prepare themselves for entering the Junior Class.

4. The completion of the Junior Course entitles the student to the degree of Licentiate of Instruction (L. I.); of the Senior Course, to the degree of A. B.; and of the Post-Graduate Course to the degree of A. M.

5. Students who have maintained themselves in the College for one or more years at their own expense, and have there maintained a high record, should have preference over all other candidates for a scholarship.

6. The applicant for scholarship must be at least seventeen years of age; must present to the President of the College a certificate of irreproachable moral character, gentlemanly or lady-like habits, and presumed good health; must declare his intention of making teaching a profession; must give a pledge to remain at the College two years, if the scholarship is continued so long; must promise to submit cheerfully to all its requirements in study, discipline, etc., and to teach in the public schools of his or her own State at least two years, if there is an opportunity.

7. Every member of the College is required to pay an incidental fee of $6 a year. Text books are loaned to pupils free of charge.

W. H. PAYNE, *President.*

NASHVILLE, TENN., February 1, 1890.

Approved: J. L. M. CURRY, *General Agent*, Richmond, Va.

DECLARATION.

(c.) I,..., of..................................... ....
was...............years old on the...?.....................day of...................................:........................18...........
My object in obtaining a "Peabody Scholarship" in the Normal College at Nashville, is to qualify myself for teaching; and for this purpose it is my intention to remain in that institution two years, if I should be admitted; and I hereby promise to teach, after I have left it, at least two years in the public schools of this State, if I have opportunity. I further promise to attend regularly and faithfully upon all exercises required, and to conform cheerfully

to the discipline and rules which may be prescribed. And should I, for any reason, fail to teach, as agreed, after graduating, I promise to refund to the President of the College an amount of money equal to that which I have received from the Peabody Education Fund.

I also promise to report myself as often as once each year to the State Superintendent of instruction for this State, either by letter or in person, for two years.

....18.........   Signed..

This declaration, and a duplicate of the same, must be signed in good faith. One will be filed in the office of the State Superintendent, and the other sent to Nashville with other testimonials.

EXTRACT FROM REGULATIONS OF THE SOUTH CAROLINA MILITARY ACADEMY.

PAR. 13.—*Moral and Physical Qualifications.*—Applicants for Cadetships shall not be less than 15, nor more than 20 years of age at the time of admission; and not under 5 feet in height. As to Beneficiaries, this rule will be strictly enforced; as to Pay Cadets, among whom there is no competition for admission, the Board of Visitors may exercise some discretion. They shall be of good moral character, free from contagious diseases, and of a physical conformation and development which will qualify them for military service.

PAR. 14.—*Knowledge Requisite for Admission.*—The standard of educational qualification to enter the Fourth Class in the Academy shall be ability to read and write English with facility, Arithmetic completed, and a knowledge of the Elements of English Grammar, of Descriptive Geography, and of the History of the United States. Upon presenting themselves for admission, either Pay of Beneficiary Cadets, may be admitted, at the discretion of the Faculty, to a higher class if found competent upon examination.

PAR. 15.—*Married Persons.*—No married person will be appointed a Cadet; and if any Cadet should be married while in the Academy, he shall leave the Institution.

PAR. 17.—*Time and Manner of Applying.*—All applications for admission into the Academy shall be addressed to the Chairman of the Board of Visitors. Pay Cadets may apply at any time; Beneficiary Cadets should apply after the Annual Graduating Exercises in June, when existing vacancies in the several Counties are announced in the County papers.

PAR. 18.—*Form of Application, &c.*—All applications for Beneficiary Cadetships in the Academy shall be made upon a printed form, which will be furnished on application to the Chairman of the Board. These applications shall be laid before the Board of Visitors, and upon approval by them, the Chairman of the Board shall forward to each applicant a permit to appear for examination before the County Board of Examiners hereinafter provided for. No one without such permit will be examined by the County Board. A Beneficiary Cadet once discharged from the Institution will not be allowed again to appear in competition for re-appointment. No Beneficiary appointment will be awarded where a brother has previously received the same benefaction.

PAR. 19.—*Competitive Examinations for Beneficiary Cadets.*—The competitive examinations, for selection of Beneficiary Cadets from the Counties, will be held at the respective County seats, and the candidates will, at as early a day as possible after vacancies are announced, make application to the Chairman of the Board for permission to appear before the examiners. There shall be selected by the Superintendent of Education three suitable persons in each County, who shall constitute the Board of Examiners for that County. Such examination to be superintended by the Superintendent of Education, and conducted under such rules as he may prescribe. The result shall be reported to the Superintendent of Education, who shall, when satisfied that the competition has been fairly conducted under the rules announced, report the results to the Chairman of the Board of Visitors. The Chairman of the Board of Visitors will forward to each successful applicant a Warrant of Appointment, who, upon receiving same, will repair to the headquarters of the Academy by such day as the Board of Visitors may fix. He will be again examined by the Academic Board and Surgeon.

PAR. 23.—*Beneficiary Cadets, on Matriculation, Give a Bond.*—Every Beneficiary Cadet, upon reporting for duty and matriculating, shall file with the Superintendent of the Academy a bond, payable to the Academy, in a penal sum sufficient to cover the maintenance and education that may be expended in his behalf, and conditioned for the faithful performance by said Cadet of his matriculation agreement to teach for two years after graduation in the free Public Schools of the State as provided by law; and if honorably discharged before the completion of his course, then to teach for a period of time proportioned to the time he has been in the Academy. And unless the Cadet shall fulfill his obligation as aforesaid, he shall be deemed to have violated his contract, and the Academy will proceed by law for the collection on said bond of such amount as may be necessary to cover the maintenance and education of said Cadet as may be proportionately due from his failure to teach the whole or any part of the time agreed as aforesaid. And neither the infancy of the Cadet executing such bond nor the Statute of Limitation can be pleaded in bar of the recovery of said debt.

PAR. 27.—No Cadet is furnished with underclothing, shoes or uniform (except the undress suit) until after a probation of three months; at the end of which time the Superintendent, with the concurrence of the Professors, shall have power to dismiss from the

Academy all such probationary pupils as shall have shown utter incapacity, or whose conduct shall have been grossly immoral, or generally improper, or insubordinate. During the whole course Cadets shall supply themselves with books, blankets and a comfort.

STANDING RESOLUTIONS OF STATE BOARD OF EXAMINERS.
REGULATIONS.

RULE 1. To find the average attendance of one school for one school month, add the number of pupils attending each day and divide the sum by twenty.

RULE 2. To find the average attendance of one school for one school year, add the averages as found by Rule 1 and divide the sum by the number of school months that the school has been in session.

RULE 3. To find the average attendance of a school district for one school year, add the averages as found by Rule 2.

RULE 4. To find the average attendance in a County for a school year, add the averages as found by Rule 3.

RULE 5. To apportion the school fund, divide the proceeds of the school tax by the average attendance of a County as found by Rule 4, and multiply the quotient by the average attendance of the several school districts. The products thus obtained will be the amounts to which the respective school districts will be entitled.

EXAMINATIONS.

Resolved, At all examinations before County Boards, at least two members of the Board must be present.

Resolved, All applicants before County Boards shall be examined on orthography, reading, writing, arithmetic, geography, English Grammar, history of the United States and of this State, physiology, hygiene, and the theory and practice of teaching, elementary algebra, elementary English literature, elementary drawing, elementary vocal music.

RECOGNITION OF CERTIFICATES GRANTED IN OTHER COUNTIES.

Resolved, That any County Board of Examiners may, in its discretion, recognize certificates of qualification granted in other Counties as evidence of qualification to teach in the public schools, without subjecting the holders of said certificates to another examination.

TIMES FOR HOLDING COUNTY EXAMINATIONS.

Resolved, That examinations by County Boards of Examiners be held on the third Friday in April and October of each year, or on such other days in those months as the State Superintendent of Education, in his discretion, may direct.

APPEALS.

Resolved, That in all cases where appeals are taken from the rulings of the County Boards of Examiners to the State Board of Examiners, notice of intention to appeal shall be given in writing by the appellant to the party or parties affected and the County Board within ten (10) days from date of hearing by the County Board, and that the appeal shall be perfected within thirty days from the date of hearing by the County Board, otherwise the appeal shall not be entertained by this Board.

Resolved, That, in future, all papers relating to appeals to be brought before the Board be required to be filed in the office of the State Superintendent of Education at least twenty (20) days before the time prescribed for the meeting of the Board.

PURCHASING OF SCHOOL SUPPLIES.

The State Superintendent is authorized to permit firms and individuals to present such of their school supplies as he approves of to the County Boards of Examiners of the several Counties of the State: *Provided,* That before he grants a permission to any firm or individual he shall require such firm or individual to deposit in his office samples of such supplies, and shall be satisfied with the goods and the prices, and require the vendor to enter into a written contract that the goods sold shall at all times conform to the samples, and that the prices shall not exceed the prices agreed on: *Provided, further,* That County Boards of Examiners may approve or disapprove of any or all such supplies, and may allow or disallow the same to be sold within their Counties. In case they approve of any of such supplies, and permit the same to be sold, they shall give the vendor a written permission to offer the same to their Trustees at the prices named by them in such written permission, leaving the purchase or not of such supplies to the good judgment of the respective Boards of Trustees.

LICENSES.

Resolved, That the regulations of this Board permitting County Boards of Examiners to issue *Licenses* in special cases be, and the same are hereby, repealed; and that hereafter these Boards be permitted to grant *Licenses* only upon examinations, permission to hold such examinations being first obtained from the State Superintendent of Education, and the Licenses so granted to continue of force up to the next regular County examination of teachers, and no longer, with the right to the County Boards issuing to revoke them at pleasure.

3—SL

RESOLUTION.

It having been brought to the attention of this Board that certificates have been granted by County Boards of Examiners on diplomas given by institutions that are not colleges nor universities, which is in violation of the proviso of Section 1005 of the School Law, therefore, be it

Resolved, That the State Board of Examiners disapprove this granting of certificates, and instruct County Boards to confine themselves strictly to diplomas from colleges and universities.

LIST OF SPECIAL SCHOOL DISTRICTS.

Special School Districts.	Extra Tax Permitted.	Estab-lished.	Amended.	Re-pealed.
Winnsboro	2 mills.	1878	1887	
Chester	2½ "	1879	1893	
Kershaw No. 1	3 "	1879	1887, 1892	
Monticello Academy	2 "	1879	1880	
Union	1½ "	1879	1882	
Johnston	1½ "	1879	1882	
Columbia	2 "	1880	1881, 1883, 1893	
Ridge Spring	3 "	1882	1888, 1889	
Varnsville	2 "	1882		
Leesville	2 "	1882	1883	
Sandy River	2, "	1882		
Blackstock	2 "	1882		
Orangeburg	3 "	1882	1893	
Walterboro	2 "	1882	1885	
Ridgeway	2 "	1882		
Little River	2 "	1882		
Florence	4 "	1883	1889, 1890, 1893	
Timmonsville	2 "	1883	1886	
Marion	2½ "	1883	1886	
Union	3 "	1883	1888, 1892	
Spartanburg	2 "	1883	1884, '89, '91, '93–6	
Mount Pleasant School Tax		1883		
Bamberg	3 "	1883		
Wilksburg	2 "	1884	1886	
Summerville	2 "	1884		
McConnellsville	2 "	1884		
Slabtown	2 "	1885	1889, 1890	
Georges	2 "	1885		
Georgetown	2 "	1885		
Greenville	2 "	1885	1893	
Martin	3 "	1885		
Allendale	2 "	1886		
Barnwell	2 "	1886		
Bennettsville	3 "	1886	1888	
Lowrysville	2 "	1886		
Marion	2½ "	1886	1894	
Blacksburg	4 "	1887	1888, 1892, 1894	
Brunsons	2 "	1887		
Coneross	2 "	1887		1888
Edgefield	2 "	1887		
Greer's	2 "	1887		
Laurens	4 "	1887	1890	
Montmorenci	2 "	1887		
Rock Hill	2 "	1887		

LIST OF SPECIAL SCHOOL DISTRICTS.—(Continued.)

Special School Districts.	Extra Tax Permitted.		Estab-lished.	Amended.	Re-pealed.
Seneca	5	mills.	1887	1888	
Soccastee	5	"	1887	....	1889
Sumter	2	"	1887	1888, 1889, '91, '93.	
Nos. 9, 19, 20, 21, Fairfield County	2	"	1887		
Broad River	3	"	1888		
Butler	No provision.		1888		
Centennial	3	mills.	1888		
Cheraw	3	"	1888	1889	
Darlington	5	"	1888	1889, 1896	
Holley	3	"	1888		
Piedmont	No provision.		1888		
Rutherford	3	mills.	1888	1891	
Williston	2½	"	1888	1890	
Yorkville	2	"	1888	1889	
General Act for	....		1888		
Fort Hill	2	"	1889		
Kershaw	3	"	1889		
Newberry	2	"	1889		
Conway	Seminary.		1889		
Bethesda	2	mills.	1890		
Bishopville	4	"	1890		
Blackville	3	"	1890		
Camden	3	"	1890		
Edgemoor	4	"	1890	1891	
Hendersonville	2	"	1890		
Shiloh	2	"	1890		
Tirzah	2½	"	1890	1894	
Wellford	2	"	1890	1891	
Laurens County (to be laid off)	½	"	1891	1893	
Abbeville	2	"	1891	1892, 1896	
Edisto River	2	"	1891		
Elko	5	"	1891		
Lancaster	5	"	1891		
Ora	3	"	1891	1893	
Ridgeville	2	"	1891		
Sally	2	"	1891	1892, 1893	
Beulah	5	"	1891		
Salem	3	"	1891		
No. 3, Berkeley County	....		1891		
Greenwood	....		....	1892	
Union (Edgefield and Abbeville)	3	"	1892		
Princeton Laurens and Greenville)	3	"	1892		
Union High School	3	"	1892		
Wheeland	3	"	1892		
Ebenezer	2	"	1892		
Little Mountain	2	"	1892	1893	
Elloree	5	"	1893	1894	
Cross Hill	3	"	1893		
Hurricane Academy	....		1893		
Neeseton	....		1893		
Swansea	....		1893		
Anderson	2	"	1894		
Waterloo	3	"	1894		

bia; W. A. Clark, Esq. (term expires 1896), Columbia; Hon. A. T. Smythe (term expires 1896), Charleston; Hon. J. W. Ferguson (term expires 1896), Laurens. *Secretary of Board.*—Isaac H. Means, A. B.

COUNTY SCHOOL COMMISSIONERS.

Elected November, 1894, and term of office expires Janury 1st, 1897.

COUNTY.	NAME.	POSTOFFICE.
Abbeville	*W. T. Milford	Abbeville.
Aiken	L.W. Williams (dec'd)	Aiken.
Anderson	*D. H. Russell	Anderson.
Barnwell	L. N. Bellinger	Barnwell.
Beaufort	James Wigg	Beaufort.
Berkeley	*A. H. DeHay	Monck's Corner.
Charleston	W. H. Dunkin	Charleston.
Chester	*W. B. Thompson	Chester.
Chesterfield	*T. Threatt	Chesterfield.
Clarendon	*L. L. Wells	Manning.
Colleton	Oliver P. Williams	Walterboro.
Darlington	*A. J. A. Perritt	Darlington.
Edgefield	P. N. Lott	Edgefield.
Fairfield	D. L. Stephenson	Winnsboro.
Florence	E. J. Smith	Florence.
Georgetown	*G. E. Herriott	Georgetown.
Greenville	*J. R. Plyler	Greenville.
Hampton	*S. J. Fitts	Hampton.
Horry	D. D. Harrelson	Conway.
Kershaw	J. A. Grigsby	Camden.
Lancaster	W. B. Bruce	Lancaster.
Laurens	James A. Madden	Laurens.
Lexington	J. D. Farr	Lexington.
Marlboro	G. W. Hearsey	Bennettsville.
Marion	*S. W. Smith	Marion.
Newberry	F. W. Higgins	Newberry.
Oconee	V. F. Martin	Walhalla.
Orangeburg	*E. H. Houser	Orangeburg.
Pickens	T. C. Robinson	Pickens.
Richland	*L. C. Sylvester	Columbia.
Sumter	*W. J. DuRant	Sumter.
Spartanburg	*B. B. Chapman	Spartanburg.
Union	M. L. Lemaster	Union.
Williamsburg	J. J. B. Montgomery	Kingstree.
York	John A. Shirley	Yorkville.

* Re-elected.

STATE BOARD OF EDUCATION.

HIS' EXCELLENCY JOHN GARY EVANS, Governor,
    ex officio Chairman..Columbia.
HON. W. D. MAYFIELD, State Superintendent of Education,
    ex officio Secretary......................................Columbia.
HON. JULIAN MITCHELL..Charleston.
PROF. W. N. MARCHANT ....Monetta.
PROF. J. I. McCAIN..Due West.
PROF. A. T. COOK...Greenville.
PROF. A. R. BANKS...Yorkville.
HON. W. F. CLAYTON ....Florence.
PROF. A. M. RANKIN..Orangeburg.

INDEX.

A.

44

45

46

48

www.ingramcontent.com/pod-product-compliance
Lightning Source LLC
Chambersburg PA
CBHW021555270326
41931CB00009B/1225